WHEN WALT DISNEY RODE A PIG

by Mark Weakland

illustrated by Pablo Pino

PICTURE WINDOW BOOKS

a capstone imprint

It was black and sticky, but that didn't matter to Walt Disney. He dipped his paintbrush into the barrel of tar. **"This would be real good to paint with,"** he told his sister, Ruth. **"Let's paint on the house!"**

Ruth dipped her brush into the tar and drew zigzags. Walt drew a house with a smoking chimney.

Young Walt had a gift for drawing and creative thinking. He worked hard. When he decided to do something, he did it. Walt's abilities brought him fame and fortune — and sometimes a bit of trouble!

Walter Elias Disney created a company loved by millions of people around the world. But his beginnings were humble.

He was born on December 5, 1901, in Chicago, Illinois. Five years later, his father and mother, Elias and Flora, moved their family to Missouri. Their new home was a small farm outside Marceline. The family lived there only four years. But they were happy years for Walt.

While Walt's mother did farm chores, Walt and his sister tagged along. In time, Walt got pretty good at herding the pigs. When the pigs grew to trust him, they let him ride on their backs.

Walt grew especially fond of one runty piglet. He named
it Skinny and fed it from a baby bottle. Skinny loved
Walt and followed him everywhere. "Come on, Skinny,"
said Walt. "Let's explore!"

Walt was 7 years old when he finally started school. He was interested in many things other than schoolwork. Because of that fact, his grades were never better than average.

One place Walt loved was the town's new movie house. "Let's go, Ruth, please!" he pleaded. Usually Ruth said no. But one day she gave in. In the darkness of the theater, the two watched a movie based on the Bible. To Walt, it was magic.

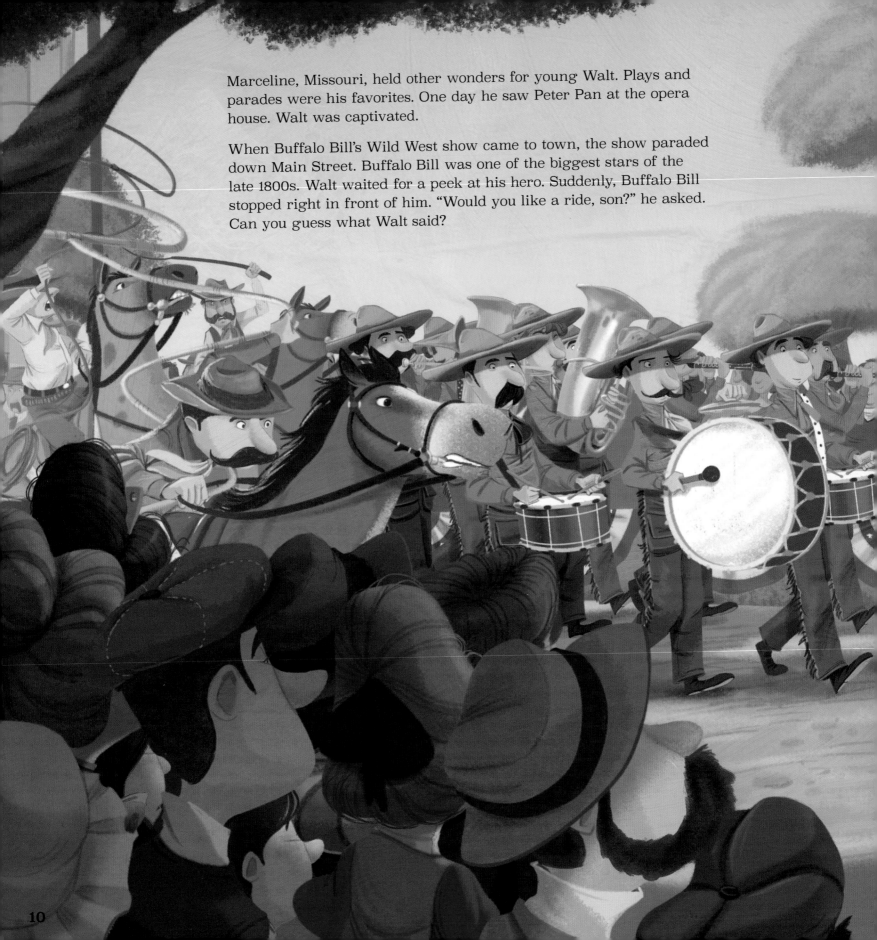

Marceline, Missouri, held other wonders for young Walt. Plays and parades were his favorites. One day he saw Peter Pan at the opera house. Walt was captivated.

When Buffalo Bill's Wild West show came to town, the show paraded down Main Street. Buffalo Bill was one of the biggest stars of the late 1800s. Walt waited for a peek at his hero. Suddenly, Buffalo Bill stopped right in front of him. "Would you like a ride, son?" he asked. Can you guess what Walt said?

Walt's aunt Margaret encouraged Walt to draw. She gifted him with crayons and pads of paper. Armed with supplies, Walt drew animals and flowers. He also drew townspeople.

One of his subjects was old Doc Sherwood. The retired doctor offered Walt a commission. "I'd like you to draw a portrait of me and my horse, Rupert," said Doc. Walt was happy to do it. For his work, he was paid one quarter.

The year 1909 was hard for the Disney family. First, Walt's two oldest brothers ran away from home. Then the farm's well went dry. Finally, Walt's father got very ill.

Walt's 16-year-old brother, Roy, tried to manage the farm on his own. But it was too much work. "I'm selling the farm," their father said. "We're moving to Kansas City." Roy and Walt were heartbroken when their favorite colt was sold to another farmer.

In Kansas City, Missouri, Walt's father got a job delivering newspapers. Walt and Roy helped. Walt picked up his papers long before sunrise. When his deliveries were done, he went to school. After school, he delivered more papers.

The papers were heavy. Walt wasn't allowed to use his bike, so he carried a bag or pushed a cart. He walked in all kinds of weather. In six years, he missed only four weeks of work.

Walt's years in Kansas City were difficult. But he still found ways to have fun. He and his friends once watched a circus parade roll through town. Afterward they decorated old wagons and made their own parade.

Another time, Walt made his sister smile when she got very sick. "Look, Ruth," he said. He showed her a small book of his drawings. Ruth flipped through the pages. The figures looked like they were moving! Nine-year-old Walt had created his first animation.

19

Walt attended Benton Grammar School. He wasn't the worst
student, but he wasn't the best either. His teacher caught him
carving his name in his desk — not once but twice! And he
got into trouble for not following directions.

One day his fourth-grade teacher asked the class to draw
the flowers on her desk. Walt drew the flowers — with faces!
Instead of leaves, he drew arms and hands.

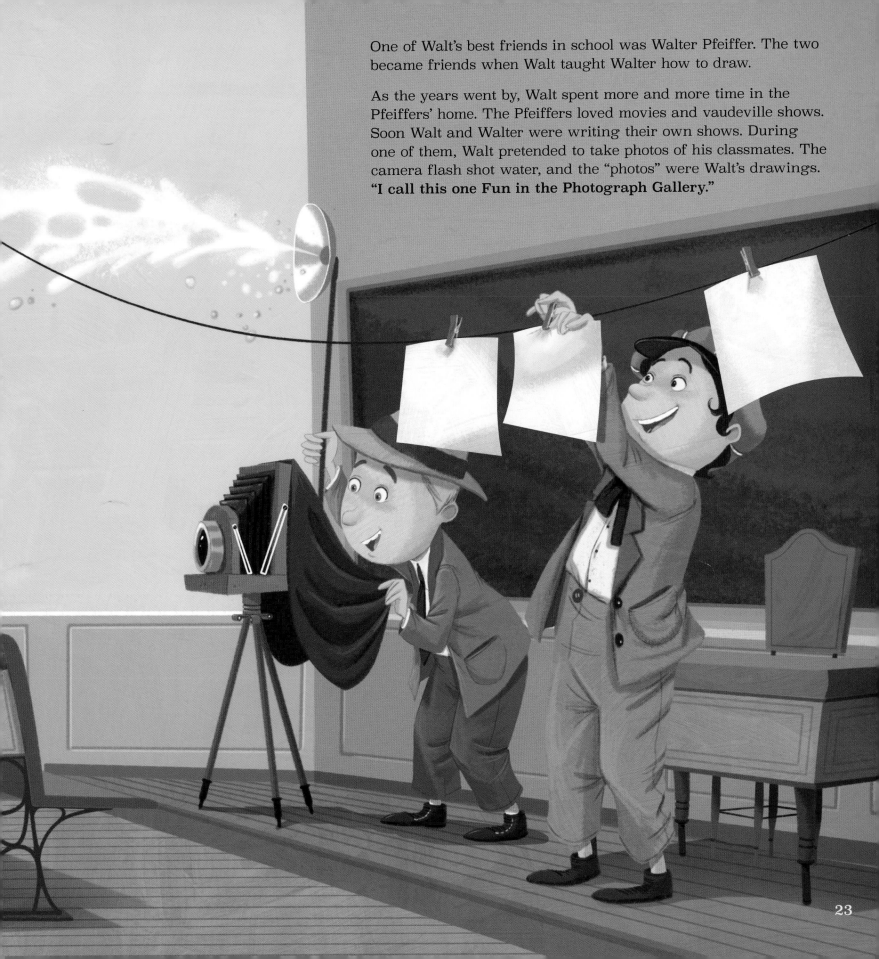

One of Walt's best friends in school was Walter Pfeiffer. The two became friends when Walt taught Walter how to draw.

As the years went by, Walt spent more and more time in the Pfeiffers' home. The Pfeiffers loved movies and vaudeville shows. Soon Walt and Walter were writing their own shows. During one of them, Walt pretended to take photos of his classmates. The camera flash shot water, and the "photos" were Walt's drawings. **"I call this one Fun in the Photograph Gallery."**

Walt wasn't sure what he wanted to be when he grew up. But then a piece of ice helped him decide.

One day while delivering papers, Walt kicked a large piece of ice. A nail, frozen in the ice, plunged into his big toe. **"Help! I'm stuck!"** Walt cried. Twenty minutes later someone finally freed him. Walt saw a doctor and had the nail pulled out.

It took Walt weeks to recover. During this time, he thought about his future. By the time he was healed, he had made up his mind. "I'm going to be a cartoonist!"

Walt went to high school in Chicago and worked on the school newspaper. *The Voice* was the first place to publish Walt's cartoons. His drawings focused on school spirit or World War I (1914–1918).

Walt also took photographs. He studied the comic strips of Winsor McCay — one of his favorite cartoonists. He took cartooning and anatomy classes at the Chicago Institute of Art. He even visited the offices of the city's newspapers. "No one works harder than Walt," said a teacher.

Hard work and a need to create would soon make Walt Disney's wildest dreams come true.

Afterword

Walt Disney started the Disney Brothers' Studio in the 1920s. His brother Roy and his friend Ub Iwerks helped him run it. *Steamboat Willie*, the company's 1928 cartoon, featured Mickey Mouse. It was the first cartoon with sound. Walt did the voice of Mickey Mouse. The movie was an instant hit. It was the first in a long string of successes.

Walt's studio made more than 100 movies, such as *Snow White and the Seven Dwarfs* and *Mary Poppins*. Many became film classics. The studio created educational films for schools. Walt also developed TV shows, including *Davy Crockett* and *The Mickey Mouse Club*.

Walt never stopped creating and working. He wanted to make a theme park that would appeal to both children and adults. In 1955, Disneyland theme park opened in Anaheim, California.

Next, Walt planned a giant park in Florida. Disney World was still being built when Walt died from lung cancer on December 15, 1966. But his love of creating magical experiences for people never died. Today, there are Disney parks in Japan, China, and France. New Disney films and shows are seen and enjoyed by millions everywhere.

When Amelia Earhart Built a Roller Coaster

When Hillary Rodham Clinton Played Ice Hockey

When Martin Luther King Jr. Wore Roller Skates

Other Titles in This Series

When Neil Armstrong Built a Wind Tunnel

When Rosa Parks Went Fishing

When Thomas Edison Fed Someone Worms

When Wilma Rudolph Played Basketball

Critical Thinking Questions

1. Name two childhood character traits or abilities of Walt Disney. Use facts and illustrations from the book to support your answer.

2. Did the adults in Walt's life try to help him become an artist, or did they try to stop him from becoming an artist? Support your answer with two pieces of evidence from the text.

3. Name two childhood events that may have influenced Walt's life as an adult. Tell why you picked these childhood events and how they may have influenced him later in life.

Read More

Hansen, Grace. *Walt Disney: Animator & Founder.* History Maker Biographies. Minneapolis: Abdo Kids, 2015.

Mattern, Joanne. *Walt Disney.* Rookie Biographies. New York: Children's Press, 2013.

Norwich, Grace. *I Am Walt Disney.* New York: Scholastic Inc., 2014.

Orr, Tamra B. *Walt Disney: The Man Behind the Magic.* A True Book. New York: Children's Press, 2014.

Glossary

anatomy—the study of the human body

animation—cartoons made by quickly presenting drawings, one after another, so that the objects in the drawings seem to be moving

Bible—a book written thousands of years ago that is holy to Christians and Jews

captivated—holding one's full attention

commission—money paid for work done

educational—having to do with teaching and learning

humble—not thinking you are better or more important than others

theme park—a group of rides, shows, and other fun activities with a central idea or subject

vaudeville—a stage show that may include comedy, music, and stunts

Internet Sites

Use FactHound to find Internet sites related to this book.

Visit *www.facthound.com*

Just type in 9781515815761 and go.

Check out projects, games and lots more at
www.capstonekids.com

Index

Special thanks to our adviser for his advice and expertise:
Tom Sito, Professor and Chair
John C. Hench Division of Animation & Digital Arts
The School of Cinematic Arts, University of Southern California

Editor: Jill Kalz
Designer: Ashlee Suker
Creative Director: Nathan Gassman
Production Specialist: Katy LaVigne
The illustrations in this book were created digitally.

Editor's Note: Direct quotations are indicated by **bold** words.

Direct quotations are found on the following pages:
page 2, lines 2–3: Thomas, Bob. *Walt Disney: An American Original*. New York:
Simon and Schuster, 1976, p. 29.
page 23, line 8: Ibid, p. 37.
page 24, lines 4–5: Ibid, p. 39.

Picture Window Books are published by Capstone,
1710 Roe Crest Drive, North Mankato, Minnesota 56003
www.mycapstone.com

Library of Congress Cataloging-in-Publication Data
Names: Weakland, Mark, author. | Pino, Pablo, 1981– illustrator.
Title: When Walt Disney rode a pig / by Mark Weakland ; illustrated by Pablo Pino.
Description: North Mankato, Minnesota : Picture Window Books, a Capstone imprint, 2018. |
Series: Leaders doing headstands | Includes bibliographical references and index. |
Audience: Ages 6–12. | Audience: K to Grade 3.
Identifiers: LCCN 2017008206 | ISBN 9781515815761 (library binding) |
ISBN 9781515815808 (paperback) | ISBN 9781515815846 (eBook pdf)
Subjects: LCSH: Disney, Walt, 1901–1966—Juvenile literature. | Animators—United States—
Biography—Juvenile literature.
Classification: LCC NC1766.U52 D5929 2018 | DDC 741.58092 [B]—dc23
LC record available at https://lccn.loc.gov/2017008206

Printed and bound in the United States of America.
010363F17